SEASONS

8 ORIGINAL PIANO SOLOS BY CAROLYN MILLER

CONTENTS

Spring in the Air

Carolyn Miller

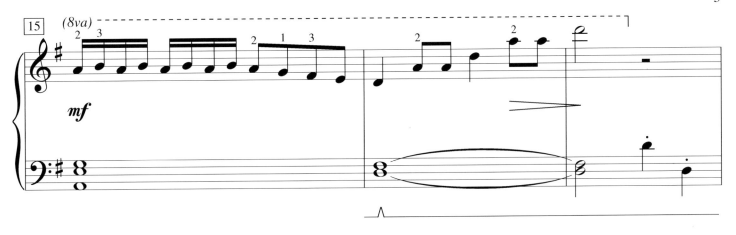

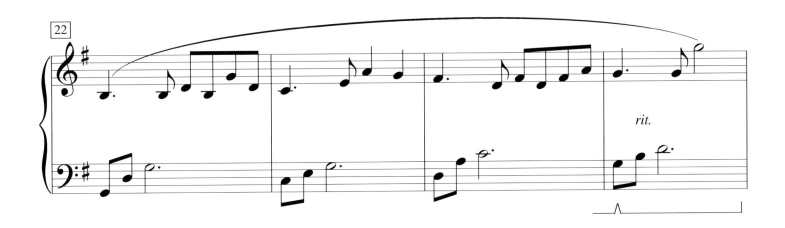

Dancing Flowers

Carolyn Miller

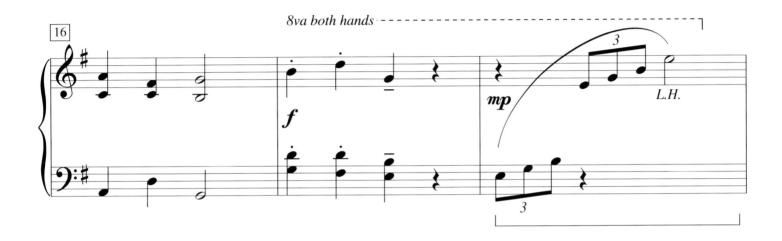

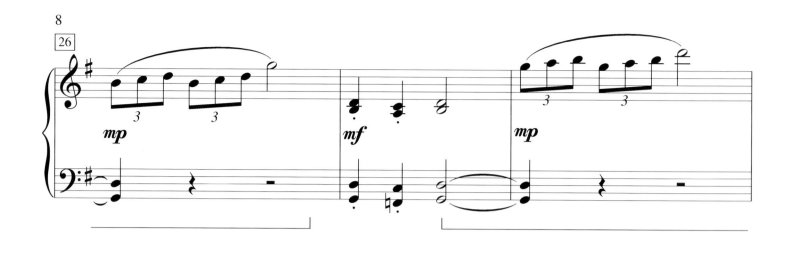

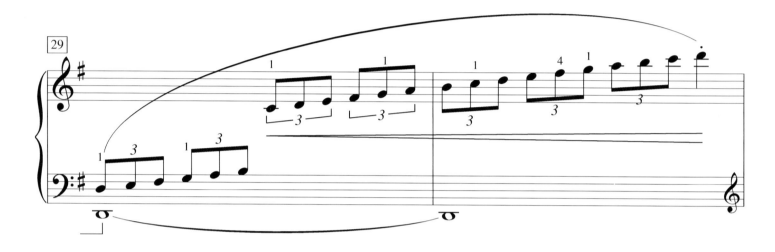

It's Summer!

Carolyn Miller

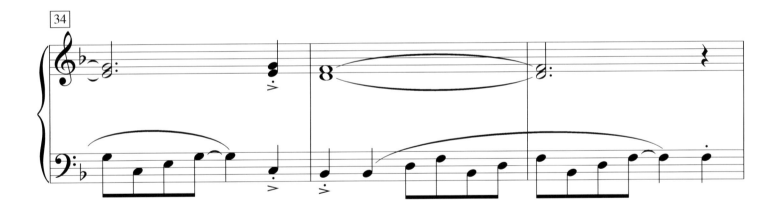

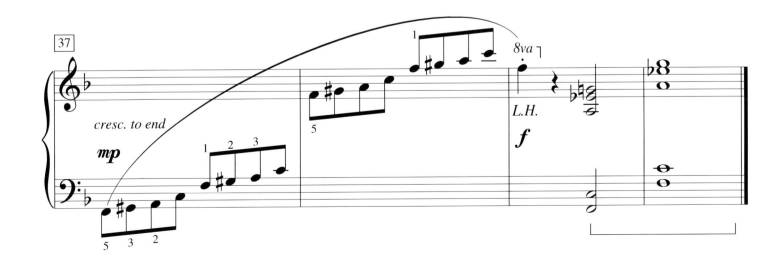

Summertime Stroll

Carolyn Miller

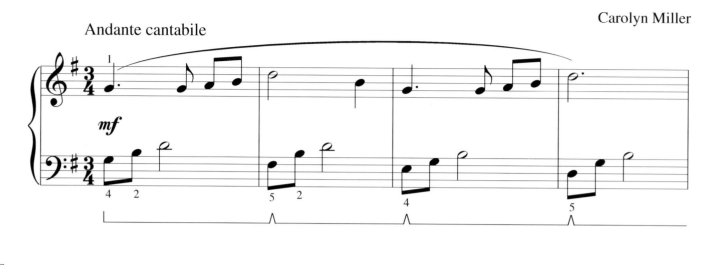

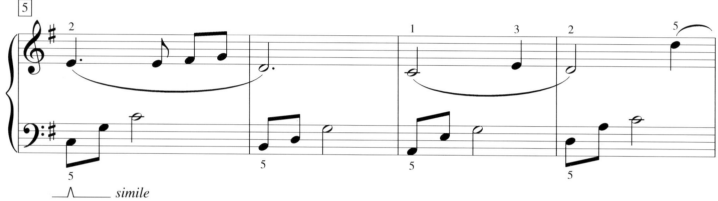

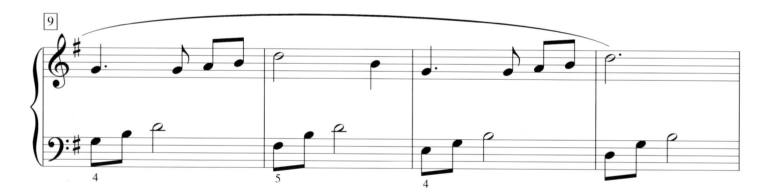

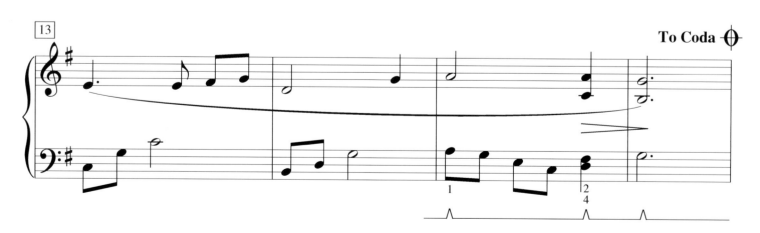

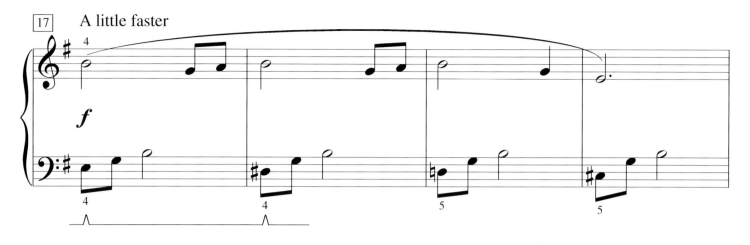

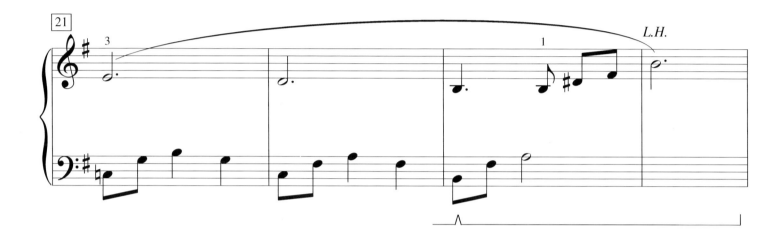

Parade of the Pumpkins

Carolyn Miller

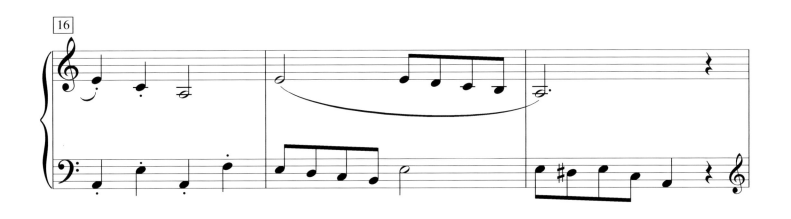

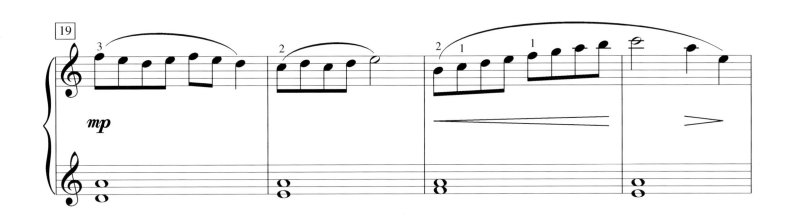

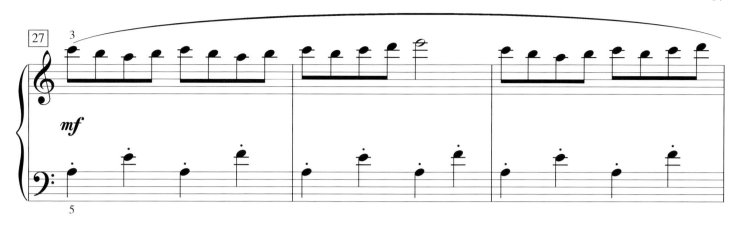

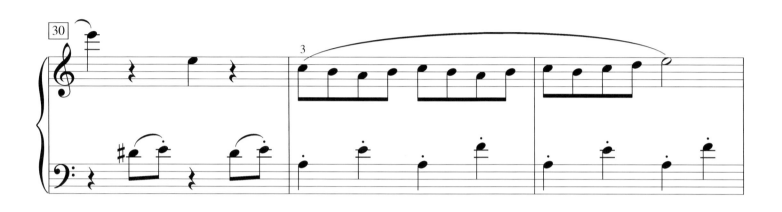

Falling Leaves

Words and Music by
Carolyn Miller

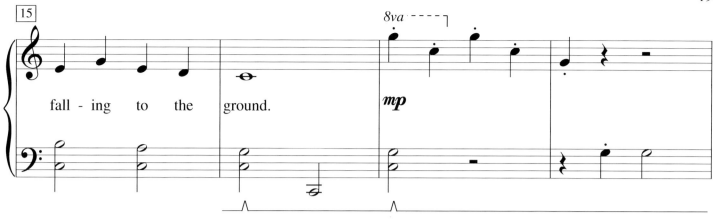

fall - ing   to   the   ground.   *mp*

Fall - ing   leaves,   fall - ing   leaves,
mf   *mp*

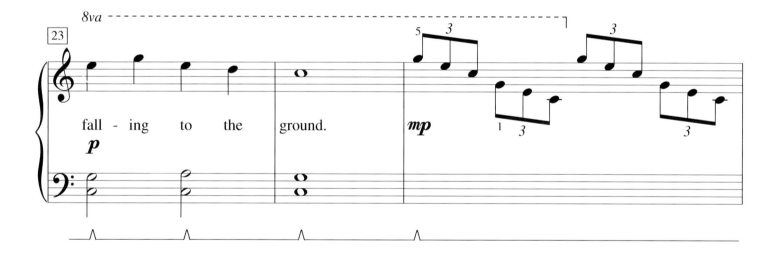

fall - ing   to   the   ground.   *mp*
p

poco rit.

R.H.

p

Cold Winter Night[*]

Carolyn Miller

---

* It is recommended that the student be taught the whole tone scale (starting on C) before beginning this piece.

Snow Skiing

Carolyn Miller

Allegro moderato

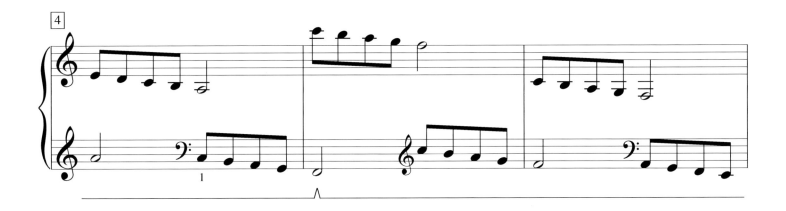

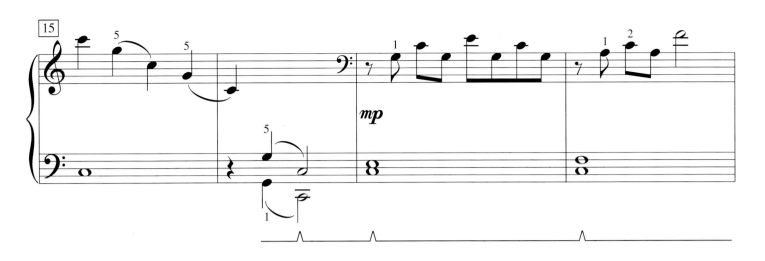

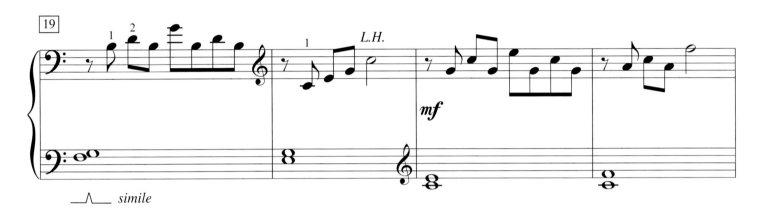

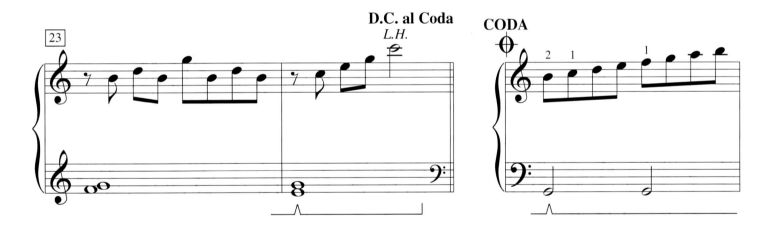

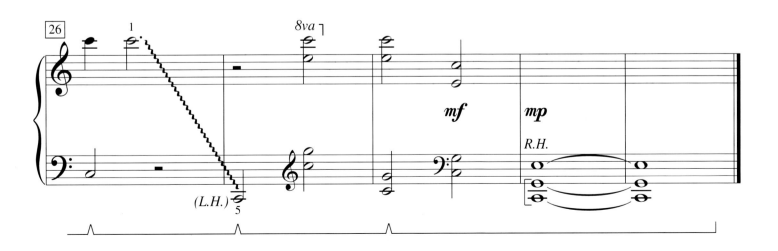

Dynamic Duets
and Exciting Ensembles from Willis Music!

SELECTED COLLECTIONS

00416804 Accent on Duets (MI-LI) /
William Gillock..........................$12.99

00416822 All-American Ragtime Duets
(EI) / *Glenda Austin* $7.99

00416732 Concerto No. 1
for Piano and Strings (MI) (2P, 4H) /
Alexander Peskanov $14.95

00416898 Duets in Color Book 1 (EI-MI) /
Naoko Ikeda $12.99

00138687 5 Easy Duets (EE-ME) /
Carolyn Miller $7.99

00406230 First Piano Duets (EE) /
John Thompson series $4.95

00416805 New Orleans Jazz Styles Duets
(EI) / *Gillock, arr. Austin*............$9.99

00416830 Teaching Little Fingers Easy Duets
(EE) / *arr. Miller* $6.99

SELECTED SHEETS

Early Elementary
00125695 The Knights' Quest (1P, 4H) /
Wendy Stevens............................ $3.99
00406743 Wisteria (1P, 4H) /
Carolyn C. Setliff.......................$2.95

Mid-Elementary
00412289 Andante Theme from
"Surprise Symphony" (1P, 8H) /
Haydn, arr. Bilbro $2.95
00406208 First Jazz (1P, 4H) /
Melody Bober.............................$2.50

Later Elementary
00415178 Changing Places (1P, 4H) /
Edna Mae Burnam $3.99
00406209 Puppy Pranks (1P, 4H) /
Melody Bober.............................$2.50
00416864 Rockin' Ragtime Boogie (1P, 4H) /
Glenda Austin.............................$3.99
00120780 Strollin' (1P, 4H) /
Carolyn Miller.............................$3.99

Early Intermediate
00113157 Dance in the City (1P, 4H) /
Naoko Ikeda $3.99
00416843 Festive Celebration (1P, 4H) /
Carolyn Miller............................$3.99
00114960 Fountain in the Rain (1P, 4H) /
William Gillock, arr. Austin........$3.99
00416854 A Little Bit of Bach (1P, 4H) /
Glenda Austin $3.99
00158602 Reflections of You (1P, 4H) /
Randall Hartsell..........................$3.99
00416921 Tango in D Minor (IP, 4H) /
Carolyn Miller $3.99
00416955 Tango Nuevo (1P, 4H) /
Eric Baumgartner $3.99

Mid-Intermediate
00411831 Ave Maria (2P, 4H) /
Bach-Gounod, arr. Hinman........$2.95
00410726 Carmen Overture (1P, 6H) /
Bizet, arr. Sartorio.....................$3.95
00404388 Champagne Toccata (2P, 8H) /
William Gillock $3.99
00405212 Dance of the Sugar Plum Fairy /
Tchaikovsky, arr. Gillock $3.99
00416959 Samba Sensation (1P, 4H) /
Glenda Austin............................$3.99
00405657 Valse Elegante (1P, 4H) /
Glenda Austin............................$3.99
00149102 Weekend in Paris (1P, 4H) /
Naoko Ikeda $3.99

Later Intermediate
00415223 Concerto Americana (2P, 4H) /
John Thompson $5.99
00405552 España Cañi (1P, 4H) /
Marquina, arr. Gillock $3.99
00405409 March of the Three Kings
(1P, 4H) / *Bizet, arr. Gillock*.......$2.95

Advanced
00411832 Air (2P, 4H) / *Bach,
arr. Hinman* $2.95
00405663 Habañera (1P, 4H) /
Stephen Griebling $2.95
00405299 Jesu, Joy of Man's Desiring
(1P, 4H) / *Bach, arr. Gillock*.......$3.99
00405648 Pavane (1P, 4H) /
Fauré, arr. Carroll......................$2.95

CLOSER LOOK

View sample pages and
hear audio excerpts online at
www.halleonard.com.

WILLIS MUSIC

www.willispianomusic.com

Prices, contents, and availability subject to change without notice.

 HAL•LEONARD®

0617